i ate a rainbow for breakfast

Joanna Crowell

Published by WordofMouth Books

Copyright © Joanna Crowell, 2012
ISBN: 978-1475241150

10 9 8 7 6 5 4 3 2 1

Printed in the United States of America

for

women writing from experience

ACKNOWLEDGEMENTS

Alexandria Ravenel, thank you for having faith in me before I had faith in me. Thank you for asking, encouraging, setting dates in stone and not taking no for an answer. It was within the embrace of your *Healing Rays Gallery* that *Women Writing from Experience* was born, and it was there—among other women writing to the heart of artichoke, with me as guide—that my own broken-heart pen found her way to rainbow.

Mom, Dad, and Nana, I am blessed beyond rainbows to have you as parents. I could not have designed on a cloud with God a more loving compassionate encouraging support system. Mom, you model for me courageous artist, flight, adventure, perpetual soul-search. For these intangibles and multitudes more, I am grateful. Dad, you model, "I can change the world! I can make a difference, and I am going to live my life working on making this world a better place for you!" Thank you for your passionate commitment to social justice and peace, and now monetary policy reform—which of course are inextricably linked. Thank you for igniting passion for justice and peace in me, and for encouraging me to write about it! Nana, you model for me commitment: commitment to family, commitment to social justice, and commitment to jumping in! You jumped in to our lives and never jumped out. Thank you for moving me to French school where I began to explore and express publicly my political views, writing (under your's and Dad's guidance) and performing speeches (that I can still recite by memory in French) on Harriet Tubman, Martin Luther King, Jr., women's rights, the threat of nuclear war—all before high school. To my parents, I am profoundly grateful for you.

To my siblings and their partners and spouses, you are the primary colors that have made my life rich, exciting, more full. Thank you for each reflection of light that you have shone on my raindrops. I cherish your unconditional love and support.

To Beki, I stand immersed in deep gratitude for your vibrant island-inspired colors, for your flowers that ooze from canvas woman-power, woman-real. Thank you for *Ascension* which not only enlivens and inspires my home walls, but also graces the cover of my first book of poems. How appropriate that she would, as she was the image that inspired the name of my first women's theatre group, *Ascension Theatre*. There is no doubt, your art has infused more color into my blood.

Angel Tyree, you embody your name. An angel you have been in my life. Some of my first adult attempts at poems were taken by your side, on your porch, in sunlight. Thank you for unwavering, powerful friendship.

Special thanks to those who have contributed in various and unique ways to this rainbow breakfast through encouragement, editing, questions, friendship. There are too many to name, but I begin: Marjory Wentworth, Tracy Isaacs, Veronica Mogyorody, Justin Deneau, Liberty Yancey, Kristen Howard-Smith, Sharon Graci, Kate Hudson, Roland Jackson, Michael Vanderhurst, Booth Chilcutt, Ed Brown, Dexter Story,

Jennifer Cormier, Unity Church of Charleston, Julian Gooding, Shannon Kennedy, Ken Luckhardt.

Sherman Evans, thank you for this cover design, and for your tireless technical assistance with so many of my artistic endeavors over the years.

To my dear friend and mentor, Kwame Alexander, thank you for holding my hand through this publishing process and sending me weekly (dreaded) deadlines! You knew I would never do it without them. You model for me Rock Star Poet, *Dancing Naked on the Floor*, and living the "writerly" life.

To those whom I have loved intimately and who have loved me—and broken me. Open. Thank you for pushing me closer to rainbow.

To the one who has grounded me, the one who has me taking more walks on the beach and spending more precious moments "in the now", the one that makes sure I eat a rainbow for breakfast every morning, even when I am groggy and grouchy, and would rather be in bed. To my son, my Neo-Love. In your words: "I love you more than what God floats on!" Thank you for being.

MENU

I.

II.

III.

IV.

I,

Love has taken away my practices
and filled me with poetry.

~ Rumi, "Buoyancy"
The Essential Rumi, Coleman Barks translation

LANDING

give me
your cheek
or forehead
or the open
stretch of
ground
between
your elbow
and wrist
on one
of those locations
I will land

HOW SHE WILL KNOW

Approach these lips
as though they were
an assignment,
a poem   yet unwritten
take your time   study
your subject matter

begin at the heart.

With soiled
calloused hands
plant the pit of a peach
(you had to devour)

Find a hammock
overlooking marsh
(hidden behind modernity)
and wait. Wait until
you have been kissed
more than three hundred times
by the South
Remember
the burn on your cheek
the sweat of your forehead
the lash on your back
the earth in your eyes
her embrace in the dark
Take note.
And wait.

Wait for
root, trunk
branch, bud
flower, fruit.

Wait until
she is
plump, round
soft, fuzzy
juice-filled
imperfect
ready.

And then,
only then
reach up
for her
with the concise
arabesque
of an aged oak
Hold your arm in the air
until it hurts.
Do not
fill your
mouth
with her
until
Emily
Dickinson
feels physically as if the top of her
head were taken off—
and no fire can ever warm her.*

At that precise moment
these lips will know
they have been
kissed.

*In 1870, poet Emily Dickinson wrote a letter to Thomas Wentworth Higginson, in it she explained: "If I read a book and it makes my whole body so cold no fire can ever warm me, I know that is poetry. If I feel physically as if the top of my head were taken off, I know that is poetry. These are the only ways I know it. Is there any other way?" (Letters of Emily Dickinson, L342a1870)

A THOUSAND SEASONS

your smile
I caught like a 24-hour flu
and in less than twenty-four hours of knowing you
food seems human and unnecessary
yet this air we share
tastes like five stars
and when you proclaim
you've known my smile
for a thousand seasons
underneath a constellation
neither one of us can name
my smile travels back
before winter   spring   summer
and falls into before
the corners of lips or teeth
had anything to do with
this revolution
like winter solstice in the South
sun returns as though it never left
now like then
I can't stop smiling
a smile only you can see
a thousand seasons, yes
times infinity
I do believe

MOMENTOUS

words flirted
wits bantered
minds met
eyes avoided

samba was our soundtrack
sushi our foreplay
the closest we got to holding hands
was the curry carrot soup we shared

a tour of the city
was our excuse
to share
the cool moist air

we sat on a bench
encircled by ocean
and there
an imaginary line
like the equator
divided our bodies
into two equal wholes
never breaking
sacred vows   souls
made
shameless love
beneath and beyond
star-speckled black

ONE KISS

between us
could never be enough
one night to shine
on a stage
would only make us want
to create more
together
one run of my hand
through your open field
could only get lost
in a forest
of never letting go
one brush of your
fingertip
against the tip of my womanhood
would only find you searching desperately
for where my mountain trail begins
and if
your expedition led
to the inlet
of my hips
you might never find your way back
to the path you have chosen
(and cherish)

so,
in these bodies
let us not share one kiss
one touch

one day
one moment to shine
let it be
this lifetime
our poems
that kiss
make love
birth babies
grow old together
let it be our poems
that explode
light up
nocturnal
skies

I REMEMBER

the dark
sweet stench
of bodies
crammed together
like the flesh
surrounded seeds
of passion fruit

I remember
the whites of his eyes
piercing through
black skin
black light
black clothes
black body
black man
he was mine.
after dark
after his mom went to bed
and his dad fell
asleep watching football
dead to the world
of teenagers sneaking through
basement windows
and dark hidden rooms
with hidden beds
and hidden acts
he was mine.
even as his stomach pushed

up against the one
with skin darker than mine
hair longer   straighter silkier
than mine

I remember
dancing
in the dark
I remember
his eyes   his hand
reaching over her   shoulder
for mine

FORBIDDEN

hidden
percussion
germinating
beneath
the melody
I hear you
faintly
like the pacing
of a cavalry
approaching
from the distance
forbidden to march
into the light
fragrant aromas
of fruit untouched
untouchable
pacify temporarily
in the shadows
in the shade
caress me
only there
the rays can wait
another moment
while you spank
the outer curves
of your djembe
and I squirm
on the inside
don't go

keeper of the rhythm
I cannot dance with you
but let me groove with you
telepathically
for a set or two
moist eyes closed
lucidly
bobbing my head
to an illicit beat
enticed by cymbals
throbbing between
the soft supple slaps
of padded mallets
flagging freedom
into light

THE SELFISH HER

wants
to dangle my
feet in his
pool
never
get wet

wants
to rent
a car
pick
him up
disable
google map
get lost

wants
to grab
his hand
join
a circus
make friends
with an elephant
walk tight ropes
meet in the
middle
fall
without
net

wants
to open
my sail
allow
his wind
to blow

My dilemma is this:

If he
got me wet
took my
hand
climbed in
became
wind

blew me
away

I would lose
all faith
that any
good
man
exists

WANT AD

cook?
clean?
do laundry?
remove boots?
eat?
sleep?

all these things
are for humans.

a poet
in love
does not
qualify
for
any
of the
above.

IN BETWEEN

it's 1:15 a.m.
2 hours past rightback
and bed begs
that I abandon gullible
to cuddle with reliable
but gullible is so desirable
yet unavailable
to rub a waitress' feet
with fragrant cocoa butter
the sticky note attached reads
rub everywhere you want me to touch
a love affair   from afar
is far from palpable
and Emerson's essays cannot edify
a naked edible breast
so instead of settling under down
I linger above comfort
hovering in between
ceiling and satisfied
Never
disguised as rightback
can suspend gravity
or paralyze a potential dream
it's hard to fall asleep
while treading air
and holding breath

CASUALTIES OF A MAN WITHOUT WINGS

he
needed big things
big metal   big tires   big freeways
to make him feel
big

but all these big things
never filled the big hole
in his chest

so he began to
torment little flying things
with no holes
and big hearts

it became a game
a way to get through long nights
of endless yellow lines

he never could
stay in the lines
he sought them out for sport
waited for them to show
their beauty   their grace their innocence

he learned their songs
studied their flight patterns
envied their freedom

made them feel like
the only birds in the universe

he waited until they trusted
his manufactured bigness
and as soon as they flew
close enough
he slammed on gas pedal
his heart racing as they
slid   maimed from his
windshield
praying to himself
that this   would be the last time
praying that these
fallen feathers
would stick to his arms
this time

HAIKU

when you speak mountains
my rivers flow, so don't talk
big   'til you can swim

HAPTIC VISION

Inspired by Laura Marks' "The Memory of Touch,"
Sigmund Freud, and feminist authors Evelyn
Glennie and Luce Irigaray.

She comes close. So close
I can no longer make out her features
I can't even tell if she's pretty or not

Move back.

How will I be able to tell if I want her
if I can't see her?

Move back.

But wait,
this feels good
I need to see her
I need to see her
What if she isn't even a her?
What if she is more like me than my eyes have
allowed me to see?
What if we have more in common
than fucking
or not fucking

I can barely make out the contour of her body
but can almost feel her skin against mine
Her touch

so gentle/so familiar/so free
It reminds me of
It reminds me of
my mother's touch.
But I can't fuck my mother

Move back.

so I can get a better look

How can I examine her with her so close?
How can I pick her apart with her so close?
How can I dominate her with her so close?
How can I turn her into object with her so close?
How can I oppress her, repress her, make her,
name her—
with her so close? How can I project
my lack onto her, with her so close?

Move back

I don't want to be reminded of what I have to lose
But this feels good. Don't want her to move back

"I am whole," she whispers in my ear

I tingle all over
her voice/her words/her skin
my skin

How will I come
to know her
with her so close?

Rely on more than my eyes?

Come closer

I can almost taste her
feel her/smell her/breathe her
hear her.

I want to know her
hold her
"Hold my hand"
We are closer

I can feel her/I can smell her
I can breathe
I hear her exhale
and can almost see her
She   can almost
see me
She can almost see me
"See me. See me."

Intersubjectively: This is a new way to see. To be.
Bringing the viewer and the viewed into proximity,
makes it hard for *one* to turn *one* into an *other.*
See?

Whispered reply: No, I don't "see"

SEEKING A MOMENT WITH MY MUSE

*I can always be distracted by love, but eventually I
get horny for my creativity.*
~Gilda Radner

I know you're busy but,
can we meet up for a moment
on a page
somewhere, on a sheet
of empty, waiting
for us
to share?

What about cyberspace?
Let's create a virtual poem
one that
denies grip
snickers at separation
ignores limitation

Meet me behind the corner candy store
Bring sweets
Let's exchange beats
rhythms
minds
Just a moment is all I seek
so, will you meet me somewhere sleek,
smooth, salty on our tongue
One grain will satisfy
my ocean cry

Meet me on the back of a camel
in the Sahara
far from responsibility
far from clock reminding
how long a second is
let's just ride
find wetness
forget history

Meet me on the tip of an iceberg
let's go north
bring your south
warm my palms
melt my insides
love my sweat
watch it glisten
know beauty

What about the bus stop?
Yes, meet me there
I will see you off
wave my poem goodbye
feel the tickle inside
the laugh you arouse
without even trying

Meet me in the tropics
beneath a grapefruit tree
together let's pick one
peel away yellow
taste ruby red
let sweet and sour
explode inside

Meet me on the outside
of a temple, church, mosque
Let's break bread
toast our communion
give thanks
know God

Meet me on a tight rope
underneath a circus tent
let's walk a fine line
between freedom and fear
hold hands
fccl safc
let go

Meet me on the wall of a cave
let's go back to before
leave our mark
our scratches
our ancient words
for some lonely soul
to discover

I know you're busy but,
just a moment is all I seek
So please, can we meet say—
somewhere, sometime?

FOG SONG

when her
thick
moist
fog
descends upon you
do not try to find
your way out
slow down
turn on your low beams
roll down the window a bit
and drive through   her
ethereal
wet
clouds
that want
only to hold you

allow her
floating
angel arms
to envelop
your vehicle
grasp your
steering wheel   lead you
to the sea

and when you
are there
standing on precipice

squinting eyes
seeing merely
hints of crest
and sunlight
(the sound of boisterous waves
the only proof you are alive)
remove your shoes
peel away your socks
roll up your pants
and walk

walk
even though
you cannot see
the edge   of her   curves
falling away from you
like sand from
a heavy man's heels
submit to her
wailing darkness
whistling
almost-painful
love droplets
into your ears
do not put your hood on
or cover your head with a scarf
allow her to chant Hare Krishna in your ear
and your eyelashes to be drenched by her wanting
    touch lashes with your fingers
taste the salt in them
smell the non-violent revolution in them
notice
how you

have changed.

walk   to the end
with her
even though
you cannot see it
and when you reach
the periphery of world
turn up the volume

and dance

dance
like a whirling dervish
in the shelter
of her mist-shadows
dance as though
all eyes have fallen
into the ocean
dance
and   listen
for what
you cannot
see

II.

For women, then, poetry is not a luxury. It is a vital necessity of our existence. It forms the quality of the light within which we predicate our hopes and dreams toward survival and change, first made into language, then into idea, then into more tangible action.

~Audre Lorde
Sister Outsider: Essays and Speeches

BLURRED BORDERS

1.
I do not know my history
I do not know
my history
My story is still being written
My story is still being spoken
My story
is a subject-in-process
a subject emerging from the object
my great great grandmother
was branded to be

This is not my story
I attempt to read jumbled letters
but words elude me
block visual field
slip out from sieve fingers
like sand falling
one
ancient
grain
at a time
disintegrated/broken-up/mixing with earth

Like slate,
your words are layered
hard
unfamiliar to me

My tongue cannot wrap around
     My mind tangled
My soul unstirred
In your words
my soul is a myth
And now that I believe
you tell me God is dead

2.
This is not   my story
I do not recognize me
within the yellowing pages of those books
Pages crack in my palms
split skin
cut down the middle
divide me from   me

Stop yelling at me!

I am not deaf or dumb
I just don't speak your language
Your language
warned my mother
that I would come out of her womb with
zebra stripes or polka dots

Were they afraid?

Pious parishioners
afraid of my father's pale fingers
mingling between those of my brown mother
before I was even conceived of
before babies were even on their minds

My father,
the presiding minister
asked to resign.

Congregation preachin'
'bout love and forgiveness and sin
And as long as her dark skin
remained on the other side of the temple
As long as she was glued to her designated pew
she was deemed worthy
to worship with thee

If only she had remained on her knees
Sang your praises
Recited your psalms
Allowed blood to clot
If only she had not crossed red carpet
If only she had believed words
that told her she was unworthy

3.
If only he
had not come down from his pulpit
If only he hadn't held her hand
If only he had known his manifest destiny
If only he had not seen her as human
If only she had been a fetish

If only my great great grandmother
had not loaded her thirteen children
with the blood of her slave master
coursing through their veins,
onto a covered wagon

If only she had taken the money offered by his son
who followed her North to bring her back to the
plantation,
in the name of his father
If only she hadn't said,

"No, I'm going up North to Freedom!"

If only my white daddy
had buckled under the pressures
of his parishioners who warned him
not to mix the colors of the rainbow

If only
he had listened to the fears of his mother
If only she had listened to the fears of her
brothers

If only colors had remained primary

I would not be here today
telling my story
Because my story has not been written
Because my story   can only be spoken
through the mixing of colors
My story
is a rainbow blurred
and must be told through fearless
performing free verse

4.
My story is a poem
and it is

peacock gold
sunset orange
lemongrass green
transatlanticslavetrade blue
soft clay red
star-lit black

My story is a blurred rainbow

If you listen closely
and dare to venture
beyond your borders
you just might find your color
in my mix.

HAIKU

even though
I'm made of sun, still I
crave her kiss each day

MAMI WATA

(for Cookie Washington, who hears the call of the Black Mermaid Goddess)

can't wait
don't wanna wait
tired of waiting
wanna jump in
swim
like Mami Wata
become
Deity
of your African waters
wanna
become one
with moon
sun
sky
grasp the shore of your existence
and pull you in

SHE SOAKS FOR HOURS

trying to relax and calm down
tells him over the phone
that she is so angry
could put her fist through a wall
They argue for an hour
as skin draws in
and grape fingers
turn to raisins
She doesn't see
her own beauty anymore

He joins her in the tub
and through fading suds
she dunks her head
and gives him head
instead of putting her fist
through a wall
like a little girl
determined to get an apple
she bobs and bobs
until he pops
She is never pleasured.
Her heart is sinking in
like wrinkles on her skin
she gets from soaking for hours
trying to calm down
and keep from crying

When she looks into the water
she cannot see her beauty

All she sees is
a limp barometer
that shrivels in hot water
just like her opinion of herself
And he blames her for it

If only she could see past his
reflection of her

CONDEMNED TO NEVER BEING NAKED

Inspired by John Berger's 1972 "Ways of Seeing,"
a BBC four-part television series

The way I slightly pucker my lips
The way I subtly switch my hips
The way I hold my chest out and shoulders back
The way I shave my underarms, legs, and crack

My every movement is meant for t(he)e
he watches me,
and I watch him
watching me.

When I wake up alone
in the morning,
look into the mirror
it is not my reflection I see
but specter that stares
back at me
I wonder how he would be
Would he turn, scream, run away?
Or would he maintain his gaze
and swear I'm beautiful anyway?
I quickly look away,
and begin to fix that
which will soon be on display

As I scour closet

for costume to impress
I am torn between tight blue jeans
and short red dress
I imagine him scoping
me out in denim
that hugs ass
in just the right way
and ponder,
will he like this look on me today?

My every movement
is meant for t(he)e
he watches me,
and I watch him
watching me.

As I rummage
through my panty drawer
I imagine him
walking behind me in the corridor
and choose the ones that dig deep
the ones that give me scars to keep

I want to wear my flats today
the ones that let me dance and play
but I choose high-heel pumps instead
the ones that help me get ahead

My every movement is meant for t(he)e
so I perform accordingly
I act as though I don't know he's there
but believe me,
I am always aware

I watch him watching me
from the corners of my eyes
From rear-view mirrors
and glass windows I surmise
My sixth sense tells me
he is in the vicinity
I can smell him behind me
and feel him beside me
I don't have to look his way
I am master at this game we play

Even when he is nowhere in sight
like when I take off all my clothes at night
still I feel his probing eyes
focused on cellulite-ridden thighs
I dim lights to avoid his penetrating praise
don't want to wake him from his dreamy gaze

My every movement is meant for t(he)e
He watches me,
and I watch him
watching me.
I am both surveyor and surveyed
The way he sees me
defines my destiny

One night,
accidentally
I saw it
and was appalled

My naked body
projected on white walls

This was not the body I wanted him to see,
the one on TV, in magazines, or nude in European
masterpieces.

I covered up immediately
with an invisible robe of insanity
condemned
to never truly being seen
by him
or by me.

UNTITLED

my
window
remains
open
for a moon
that never
comes
in

A CONFLAGRATION OF THE SCALP

Sittin' in a chair
at the Total Hair Care
head immersed in the shampoo bowl
listening to the screams.
You must have been scratchin' girl!
As she shouts for her momma or her grannie
to rescue her from chemical warfare
going on in the curls of a little girl
Toes curlin' up
Nails diggin' in to the skin of the shampoo girl
for moral support
like she was holdin' on to the hand of her man
during a contraction
Yelpin' for a hose to extinguish blazing flames
but wanting more than that,
the extinction of nappiness
and the evolution of smooth
silky silky soul sheen
of flowing beauty queens
flyin' farrah-fawcett-free
flippin' bangs out of her face.
Straight.
As straight as a priest molesting little boys
trying to be something he's not
Or was it his dad who wanted him not
to want another man?
Or was it her mom who couldn't withstand
the comb breaking in her hand?

That girl had to have been scratchin'!
Scratchin' like four little girls
on their way to Sunday school
one morning in September?
Opening up pores
for white cream
to burn brown scalp
like white hooded robes
burning churches in Birmingham
Screams continuing
Black women waiting for hours on end
Like getting our hair done
was our second part time job
Workin' overtime
gettin' paid way above minimum wage
gettin' paid with waves for days and days
Shirley temple curls
Twisted mountainous sculptures
of red purple blue blond weaves
cascading down like streams
and piled high like pyramids
Egyptian Queens talkin' about,
Oooh this humidity is terrible on my hair
My bills ain't been paid, but they can wait
'cause my 'do has got to be laid!
And I over here spending
my last dime to avoid a frizzy new growth hair line
reminding me of the time
I finally learned how to drive
a car with a manual transmission
My sister had been unsuccessfully
teaching me for weeks
but I had a hot date that night

I had to look tight
Her 1979 Honda Civic
had been sitting in the driveway for days
She was away on tour,
and I had a hair appointment.
Determined, I fumbled to find the ignition
The clutch popped
and I jerked all the way up to the beauty shop
Rolling backwards at every stop
Getting my hair done transcended my fear
of learning how to drive a stick
Vanity was my driving force,
my Hoke chauffeuring me like Miss Daisy
up Oakland hills and through Berkeley traffic.
Putt-puttin' the last mile back to my street
but my hair was lookin' as sweet
as homemade pumpkin pie
arriving in one sumptuous piece.

I have been able to drive any
manual transmission standard stick shift
ever since.

GRACE

There is no agony like bearing an untold story
inside you
~Zora Neale Hurston

pretty girls
so-so girls
skinny mini toothpick girls
one overweight girl
yuppie buffy the vampire slayer blond girls
colored girls, who have considered suicide
when the rainbow is…
troubled girls
subtle girls
with scrambled brain cells
expressions do not tell
of inner anguish
plaguing endless minutes
some eyes closed
holding back tears
others flow
some make light conversation
in between electric shocks of thought
others try laughing it off

interruption

Ms. Clark
Ms. Al-Jaber
Ms. Bernstein

on loudspeaker
amplified for entire world to hear
an obnoxious buzz
to let you into a door
where you will enter a mother
and be buzzed out a murderer
or a   survivor.
not of the fetus
but of the spirit
sleepy girls
solemn girls
slouching girls
teenybopper middle school girls
so many girls
one man.
holding her hand
eyes not wanting to meet
too ashamed
so they retreat
why me?
how could I have been
so stupid? Stupid!
I hate him
he did this to me
I told him to use a condom
but he couldn't get it up
and I wanted him to feel like a man
so I let him enter me…

Ms. Walker.

so now I must go face
my own mistakes

because hands may be held
and tears may be shed
but it is I who must lie back
with legs spread wide
altering destiny
for all of eternity
in a few moments
of moans and groans
hurting more in my mind
than in between thighs
hurting more in my heart
because I never wanted to end beginning
before start.
tears trickle down swollen cheeks
as I close eyes
bid farewells and apologize
how I agonized at the thought
of saying this goodbye
breathe. breathe.
hold on tight
gentle microscopic entity
go softly
I love your possibilities
and maybes and should haves
and shouldn't haves
(and I wish
I could have.)
I love your brave lessons
that swam through mazes
to crack open   my hard shell
I love you
I go with you
I let you go in love

for you   for me
and for children who need me
thank you angelic creature
I promise I will never forget
your gift
I cherish it with all that I am
and then
I close my legs   open my eyes
look up to the most high
and ask for forgiveness and grace
from my deepest place
and ask for grace
Baby Grace,
that will be
your name.

ABNORMAL

A routine pap smear. No symptoms appear. Yet
voice. On phone. Tells me. I have dysplasia.
Abnormal cells on my cervix. More testing is
needed. Absence of pain allows procrastination.
I mean the cells on my cervix don't hurt. But
the $700 biopsy called colposcopy confirms that
they are abnormal. And not normal, is not good.
Could lead to cancer they say. But I am a "self-
pay." So, I procrastinate.

Nurse's curse words damn carefree days, until
I make an appointment. Because what is more
important than my health. My life. How will I
change the world, if I'm dead?

The doctor asks if I am allergic to anything. I say,
"Yes. Procedures like this!" I am allergic to nice
balding men with warm smiles and cold rubber
gloves seeing me for the first time naked from
waist down. He gets to see my coochie 'cause
he's got an M.D.

and could save me.

Scoot down closer. Closer to steel speculum.
Closer to foreign fingers mingling in pink private
flesh. Prodding, stretching. Legs strain to remain
agape. Like I'm pushing hundred pound weights
on nautilus machine. Inner muscles quiver. I

cover eyes with one hand, and clench stomach
with the other. The way I do when I'm peer
pressured into riding a rollercoaster. He hears my
muffled screams and gently asks if he is hurting
me. Like a wounded puppy I whimper, "No.
Ouch. No."

The prick of sharp object on cervix in order to
numb, is as painful as the prick of needle on
thumb. But thighs spread wide, and strangers
eyes seeing parts of me I've never seen, is as
traumatic as the first day of school for a shy
little girl. I plug ears to not hear machines that
sound like loud drills scraping away a layer of
my womanhood. Cells that are no good. Pieces
of me. I cry when I am left alone with a white
paper napkin scarcely covering my nakedness and
mourn the loss of my abnormalness. And wonder
if I am normal now. The room around me is still,
and smells of KY jelly.

MY BURNING VAGINA

If you're like me, and you don't want to think about vaginas. If you're like me, and you don't want to think about your own vagina in particular. If you're like me, and you don't even like the word vagina, and never have, if it's a word that you prefer not to think about, say, see, smell, or hear. If you are avoiding contact with, acknowledgment of, and thoughts of any form of 'vaginaness'—then whatever you do, don't read *The Vagina Monologues*! And definitely don't read *The Vagina Monologues* right before you go to bed. Or like me, your dreams may be invaded by little G.I.-Vagina-Jane action figures parachuting into your consciousness like your mind is enemy territory, and you are being held captive by vagina-awareness-terrorists. Vagina thoughts in the thousands dressed in camouflage. Non-violent vagina protesters carrying bullhorns chanting, "One, two, three, four, love your vagina forevermore! Five, six, seven, eight, vagina power activate!" Vulvas and clitorises ejaculating liquid cannon balls into the air..."

Vaginas, vaginas, everywhere!

It's not fair, I can't sleep. I came to university to forget about my vagina, not to be reminded that I have one! How dare I be required to read *The Vagina Monologues* as a part of my women's studies course. I'm back in school to forget about vaginas all together. At thirty-five years old, living at home with my parents, after leaving the father of my child for allegedly visiting a vagina other than my own, the last thing I want to think about is vaginas! Let alone my own dark-down-there! I mean, I share a bedroom wall with my dad and stepmother for God's sake; I have no business thinking about anything even remotely close to my vagina. I hate vaginas! I hate thinking about vaginas. I hate reading about other people's vaginas, because when I do, it makes me think about my own. And I don't want to think about my vagina! I've been doing a damn good job of forgetting about my vagina, and forgetting about the vagina he was visiting behind my vagina's back.

You see, when I think about my vagina, I tend to think about...yep, you guessed it—sex. And when I think about sex, I think about my ex. And I just don't want to think about this stuff, and I don't want to feel all of this stuff! I have gone to great lengths to separate myself from that part of myself. I've been nursing my baby for almost two years now, and nipples that were once synonymous with sexual inspiration are now virtually numb to sensation, and purely a source of nourishment for him. And that's the way it should be!

Okay, okay it's not that I really hate vaginas per say, and I don't actually hate my own vagina. I do appreciate all of the biologically practical functions it performs and all. What I hate, is this pain that I feel in the deepest, darkest, most private part of my insides. Pain that is as vulnerable as a vagina waiting, wanting, throbbing to be entered for the first time, but is terrified. Pain that is as plain, and as straightforward, and as descriptive as the word itself: vagina. Pain that is as raw, and as sore, and as tortured as a vagina that has been mutilated in the name of tradition, in the name of religion, in the name of God. Pain that is as sore and as tender and as open as a vagina that has stretched wider than a grand canyon to allow new life to emerge from her. Pain that was ignored when she shouted, "No! Stop. No!"

Pain that is as pink, and swollen, and torn-up as a vagina that has surrendered for passion to probe her soul, over and over, until ecstasy transcends. And the vagina, and the penis, and the ego no longer exist. Pain that is as bruised, and as battered, and as buried as a vagina that has been betrayed by the source of her greatest high. Pain that aches for just one more hit, just one more kiss, just one more union with that one. Pain that cries dry tears that burn, and turn her pink into bright red.

I see.

A bright red hot sun burns inside me. And She. Is what. Keeps me. Alive.

I ATE A RAINBOW

for breakfast
swallowed the moon
whole for dinner
(skipped lunch
to occupy
your heart)
dreamt
a new
world
'til the sun
rose from
inside
me

III.

There can be no love without justice.

~ bell hooks, Feminism is for Everybody: Passionate Politics

REACH

deep
down
in between
the   lines
of the words
on this page
in between words
that come/creep/launch
out of my mouthing lips
my sashaying hips
my semi-smile
my Michelle Obama style
my Harlem shake
my tour jeté
my Grace Kelly
fall
I reach
for Alvin Ailey
to squeeze me back
through the cracks of polished ash
cinder/propaganda/blame
That evil prima donna pushed me down!
down
I reach up
in between chasms of minds that divide
my left wing from her right wing
his west bank from her gaza curves
the east side from the south side of broad street
my black side from my white side

my inside from my outside
I reach for answers
from God
my mom
and google.com
Answers from them
to questions like:
What is my favorite color?
Am I pretty, smart?
Is my ass too wide?
Are my legs too short?
Am I too old to dance for you?

By age of four, I would ask
why we war for peace
Do I deserve that one piece of caramel
on the top of my daddy's shelf in his bedroom
closet, hidden
Do I deserve to reach my right hand up past ties,
like our lady of liberty
reaches beyond her nation's lies
toward the perfect constellation of my vision of
success
where seven angels fill my empty tin can
with sweet caramel inspirational fluid
igniting the heavens with freedom crème brûlée
I extend my leg
and point my toe toward the target
I quest to conquer
with love
Because bodies gliding across dusty floors
heal bare feet
protruding stomachs

Flesh entwined with flesh
like vines of a tree meshed,
feed hungry children in Somalia
I dance for hungry adults in the US of A
starving country
striving to reach the moon again and again
when we won't extend health care to all of our
citizens, friends
We keep reaching higher and higher
never reaching past glass ceiling, we crash
into oblivion and become numb to toxic
microscopic falling particles
I dance to awaken
to shake
to make a difference
I dance to scatter harmful matter
and split through to the crotch
of what really matters
I dance to matter.
I dance to connect my mind
to my body to my spirit
to her waist to his back to your dance
I dance to reach
the dance in you
and you and
you.

NOT IN MY BACKYARD

I am not your city
I am not your community
I am not your neighborhood
I am not your backyard

I am not your earth
that you suspect sustains you and yours
I am theirs
so you dump on me
to protect your own
babies

and tonight I cannot sleep

under covers
under sheets
under layers of socks
cotton   toxins fleece
I freeze   tremble shriek
in silence as you scatter
invisible uranium all over me
my head feels
crushed by weight
bones ache
protruding through skin
I am thin and hungry
even though I just ate
I want to vomit
I am dripping wet

and my sweat
smells like old meat
my breasts are sore and full
full of milk
that is full of your landfills
your waste
and while you play golf
I famine and lie here shaking,
waiting
knowing soon my baby will cry
and will need me to provide
him with the nourishment you dropped
your PCBs into. Not caring one bit
about the plight of my brown baby
or me

you forgot that he
is also your baby
you forgot that I am also your mother
your sister, your grandmother
you forgot that we are connected
and that white picket fences
cannot separate dirt from dirt
you forgot that my arms
wrap around all of you,
and that I am your earth too.
I am your city, I am your community
I am your neighborhood, I am your backyard
I am your dirt

And you did not
take care of me
So tonight

I am sick
and cannot
sleep

*"....the broad array of environmental burdens
and hazards are being borne disproportionately by
lower-income communities and by racial and ethnic
minorities. Efforts to address this concern have been
given the label of environmental justice..." (IOM,
1999). Learn more about environmental racism
and the environmental justice movement at: www.
cwpe.org. Also see "Women of Color, Environmental
Justice, and Ecofeminism." by Dorceta E. Taylor in
Ecofeminism: Women, Culture, Nature. Ed. Karen
J. Warner (1997).*

DOUBLE DUTCH

Wake up…Wake up…
God is waking me up again!
It is 3:35 a.m., and my mind and soul
are racing. On your mark, get set, go!
I try to go…back to sleep!
But God persists as I resist
Get up and write this down
So often we miss God's wake-up calls
count make-believe sheep
attempting forced sleep
as the gun of life repeats
Pop! Pop! False start, go back to bed.

But sometimes it is so loud and clear
that it is God pulling the trigger
we jump up and heed even fatigued
because we know that it is She/He
We know it in the breath we breathe
We know it at the tips of the hair of our arms
standing
facing up toward heaven

I know it. After a long day at work
and I'm feelin' like Pinocchio without Geppetto
wooden wobbly legs bucklin' at the knees
scarcely makin' out to the street—
when an angel puppeteer
miraculously tilts my head up to the sky
just as the sun dives

into cotton candy purple clouds
in slow motion
In that moment I am revived, alive
telling the truth

That no man could have produced
such brilliance of mismatched
perfectly blended swirls of shapes and colors
Yet in my bed at 4-oh-I-don't-know-a.m.
I am contradicted by bland apartment walls
whispering in my ear
but look over here at your sister Beki's painting
illuminating waning white
like the crown of a new born king
exiting its virgin mother's womb
or like perigee moon the darkest of nights
and once again I know that it was God
and she had to have known it was God
Sometimes we just know
like Michelangelo, or Maya Angelou
And when we do know why the caged bird sings
we get up and write despite our burning eyes
because we know God is gonna
guide our pen across—
I pause.

My ego gets in the way of God so many times
because it doubts and says, "Yeah, right!"
and the flow is interrupted by me
myself and I. But it never blinds God's eye
In me/is me/can and will never leave me
My side, my inside
All of the crooked crazy sides of Joanna

God is there. God is in the air
God is in this ink
black on white (like me)
stretched across blue lines
that I have drawn between
me and She/He

Waking up
to erase/blur/concur
that I am jumping rope
with that line
connecting the spaces
you holding one end
God at the other
and I am jumping high
so high, 'cause when I recognize
that it is God waking me up
I don't, I can't miss a beat
I can double Dutch with the best on the street
I am that little girl from Brooklyn
who's been jumpin' since she was three
We are one. God, Michelangelo, Maya, Beki,
the newborn king, the double Dutch queen and
me!
I jump higher and higher. Free. And awake.
My soul wins the race.

Thank God,
now I can get some rest!

I JUST WANT TO BE A MOM

*I loved you before I saw the kingdom in your
tummy.*
~Neo (4 years old)

Right now,
I don't want to write
I just want to be a mom.
Today,
I don't want to be an artist,
a poet, an actress, or a superstar
I just want to be a mom.
This week,
I don't want to facilitate a writing workshop
on self-esteem, as I struggle to find my own
I just want to feed my baby boy,
and pat and rub his back until he burps
Oh, the joy of a newborn's burp.

For a little while
I don't want to figure out what to do
with the rest of my life,
I just want to be a mom.
For a minute,
I don't want to be an activist
I just want to be a mom.

On this page,
I don't want to write a poem,
I just want to be a mom.

I could never write a poem
as powerful and painful as a contraction.
I could never write a poem as warm as his
body resting against mine.
I could never write a poem
that smells as sweet as his spit up.
I could never write a poem
as peaceful as his first smile.
I could never write a poem as curly and wild
as his hair that gave me heartburn for months.
I could never write a love poem that burns
as much as my heart does now.
I could never write a poem   as innocent as he
I could never write a poem
as innocent as he

By the time I could write
I wrote out of need
I needed to write
to fix something broken in me
He is not broken yet
by society
a broken marriage
a broken heart
a broken country.
He is whole
at six weeks old
More whole than I,
though he needs me
even to hold his head up.

On this day,
I just want to hold my baby's head up,

and stare back into his black eyes
Black eyes that do not look away
Black without shame.
He stares at me
through me
past my shame
past my flaws
past my insecurities
past my pain
all the way to my innocence
all the way to my joy.

In this moment,
I just want to be like him—

Enough.

YESTERDAY I WAS KING

(for Roland)

1.
That day he played like every other day
He played in restaurants, at bus stops
on trains, in airports, on the plane
and only one complaint was ever made
Instead of turning around and politely asking
himself, a man in a stiff suit
had the flight attendant attend
to his dirty work. Was it long locks he dreaded,
or hershey extra dark that made him feel milky weak?
He claimed he needed to get some sleep
The gentle music man tapped on stiffsuit's
shoulder to let him know that he would gladly
oblige his request. Stiffsuit turned around
and as swift as a whip said, "Why don't you just
put your thumb in your mouth!"

2.
A man
scolded like a toddler
A king
yesterday. I was.
lashed back
with thumbs
not in mouth
but on tips of steel strips
Thumbs not tucked under into fist

but extended outward
plucking peacefully, ferociously
away at his kalimba
a tribe's first language.

Drums, jdembes, mbiras
were stripped away from men and women
like Mandela's freedom, like sewing up vagina
like binding feet, like shrouding faces
like raw meat tossed into freezer
for men to feed on later
stacked one on top of the other
in rows, on ships
without their instruments
wrists chained
thumbs contained
rhythms left behind like
treasure buried
in red-clay dirt
dirty dirt. dirty work.

3.
In the air
a Rastafarian played his kalimba
on and on round and round
as close to stiffsuit's
ear as he could get.
And drums pound on
Songs chant on
The heartbeat of
stolen brothers and sisters
lives on in the heart of a man with a kalimba
flying high above ocean of bones

communicating still
peace. Pacifying
like salty breeze.

4.
Pacify me.
Give me a thumb
Give me a thumb
to suck away my pain
to play away dirty work
Give me back my thumb
and I will stick it in my mouth
like a newborn missing the warmth
of his mother's womb
sucking away pain of a new way,
of a new home. Give me back my
first words, my kalimba
my mbira, my jdembe
and I will play away
dirty ways.

TROY DAVIS

civilized. we?
22 years; 4 stays; 4 hours. today?
i am innocent. not?
i didn't have a gun. possible?
7 witnesses recant. irrelevant?
one less nigger on our streets. please?
one less nigger to feed. yes?
people protest in the streets. futile?
a mother got some peace. true?
justice. served?
god have mercy on our souls. will she?
continue to fight this fight. we will.

(Written September 22, 2011)

A SEEMINGLY SIMPLE ACT

"When we plant trees, we plant the seeds of peace and hope."
~Wangari Maathai (April 1, 1940- Sept 25, 2011)

To plant a tree,
a seemingly simple act
is an act that can change the world.
The world of an impoverished woman,
a rural peasant farmer
who once had to walk an entire day
to fetch fuel wood for her family
in order to provide them with a nourishing meal
a meal that sometimes never came
because the wood was too far away
or because the wood did not exist.

To plant a tree,
a seemingly simple act
is an act that can save a land from soil erosion,
from desertification, and from deforestation.
It is an act that can replenish
that which has been felled
that which has been robbed
to nourish the bellies of big business men
who fill their pockets with profits
far away from the empty
holes they left behind
for natives to figure out what to do with.

To plant a tree,
a seemingly simple act
is an act that can empower an individual,
a community, a country
with self-determination,
with tools, with education, with employment,
with their own seeds,
with their own tree nurseries,
with their own fuel wood,
with pride in their own environment
and their own land.

The planting of one tree,
a seemingly simple act
is an act that can bear many fruit,
feed many hungry stomachs,
and can satisfy many longing mouths.
Mouths that long for more than just sweet nectar
but mouths that long for sweet justice
mouths that long for sweet independence
mouths that long for sweet sustainability

Oh, "idealistic" Kikuyu woman,
from the hills of Nyeri, Kenya, Africa.
Oh, woman. real. black. beautiful
with the white smile that is as expansive
as the equator that runs across your country,
dividing it into two nearly equal halves
Oh, daughter of a peasant farmer
Oh, mother of three children
Oh, first African woman to earn a Ph.D.
in Eastern and Central Africa
Oh, biological scientist

Oh, winner of the 2004 Nobel Peace Prize Award
Oh, member of parliament
Oh, Assistant Minister for the Environment
Oh, Sister Wangari Muta Maathai
In your address to the Nobel Peace Prize
Committee
you insisted that, "Those of us who understand
the complex concept of the environment have the
burden to act."

Your seemingly simple act,
your enthusiasm, your tenacity, your commitment
your wisdom, your creativity, your inspiration
your unwillingness to take no for an answer
your grassroots movement
your Green Belt Movement
your seemingly simple act
has mobilized a nation
of mostly poor rural women
to plant over 40 million trees
one seedling at a time.

To plant a tree,
a seemingly simple act
is an act that can indeed
change the world.

(Written in Fall 2005)

*See www.greenbeltmovement.org, and learn
more about Wangari Maathai and her Green Belt
Movement.*

I NEED TO BE TOUCHED

by a hand
that is human
worshipped
by fingers
other than
my own
I want a massage
I don't have to pay for
with heartache
applied pressure
to relieve centuries of stress
thumbs to play my African piano
and pluck my mbira
soothing bird songs
of ancient handheld instruments
to fill the hollow in my tree
give me circular sounds
to rub temples
round and round
on a picnic
let's go
in a basket pack
my bundle of nerves
wrapped in masculine
warm round chill bumps,
like womb round fetus
safe place to grow
and when I am reborn
give me a thumb

to stick in my mouth
so I can suck away the pain
of a new way
of a new home.

DEAR HAITI

What a powerful legacy you—
now considered the poorest country
in the Western Hemisphere—
hold in your yearning bosom
in your parched earth
in the salt of your ocean breeze
in your deforested mountainsides
in your impoverished, embattled people
in your endless cry for democracy,
dignity, independence, and peace
in the bitter taste
left on silenced tongues.

What a powerful legacy you hold

within the deep-reaching roots
of your few remaining ancient trees
within the rich mahogany of your people's skin
within the hearts of your children
who maintain hope,
remember freedom fighters,
and recite by memory the words
of Toussaint L'Ouverture
leader of eighteenth century slave revolts,
which led to the breaking of chains
and the first free Black republic.

When the French captured your Toussaint
and left him in a prison to die, he proclaimed that,

"In overthrowing me, you have cut down in Saint-Domingue only the tree of liberty. It will spring up again by the roots for they are numerous and deep."

These roots live on
in your children
these roots live on
in our children
these roots live on
in me.

(Poem written before the earthquake)

*Quoted by Paul Farmer, in "Who Removed Aristide?" London Review of Books, Vol. 26, No. 8, April 2004. Farmer, physician and founder of a free healthcare clinic in Haiti, explains that Haitian children are familiar with, and proud of their history—all reciting by memory Toussaint L'Ouverture's inspiring words.

QUOTATION MARKS

*The work of art which I do not make, none other will
ever make it.*
~Simone Weil

She's copping my style. Cloning my imagery.
Quoting my quotes. Neglecting the formality
of the quotation marks. Omitting the legality of
the bibliography. I share with her my newest
piece, and by the end of the week, I'm hearing
me, and my idiosyncrasies all up in her poetry.
Thieving themes from my anthologies. Inhaling
the Mic before me—so I end up lookin' like the
Clinton wanna-be druggie. Do I need a neon
copyright sign before I recite my freshest insights
on the Mic, or on the phone in my home to my
"homegirl?" I see you watering your vocabulary
and emoting uninhibitedly, but would you plant
your weed seeds in your own plot please! 'Cause
my high grows organically. A sober mind seeking
originality. Does it take insanity to create a new
reality? "One draw" to get closer to "one love"?
Like if I invent the latest mess-your-head-
up phrase that pays, free verse, haiku, simile,
soliloquy, screenplay—new way to make you
"holla!" Will I be more worthy of love then?

See, I'm copping her copulation. Knocking off
his name brand. Drawing strong from her weak.
Quoting his and her quotes. Neglecting the
formality of the quotation marks.

Because melodies influence subliminally. In Ella's scat. Lena's storm. Billie's southern trees. Even in the beginning there was word, and word was sound. Waves bowed cello rocks, like Romeo to Juliet, birds serenaded mates from mountaintops. Martin's preachin' 'bout having a dream, as I Michael Jordan slam dunk in my hoop dreams are contagious, and I'm catching Michael Jackson's moon in my walk. Do you want to be like Mike, too?

Nikki Giovanni expresses individuality, poetically, politically speaking Sojourner her truth. But ain't I a woman too? Giant personalities sneak out of me like dwarfs in ways I'm not even aware of. Like how I always said I would never be just like my mother, and one morning woke up in her skin! And actually liked it. I can now see that she embodies all I want to be. Her blood soars free through me. If only Elvis Presley could have seen that black polish stained through his veins when he (allegedly) said all a negro could do for him is buy his records and shine his shoes. Could it be he overheard his shoeshine "nigga" singing the blues and produced *My Blue Suede Shoes?*
Just a conspiracy theory.

Hey, could Alexander Graham Bell's best friend have put a bug in his ear, and then the telephone appeared? Just speculating. Rappers, prolific poets, portrayed as thugs and crack heads. Beautiful minds. Institutionalized. Did Jesus really have blue eyes?

Does it really matter? If I copped his attitude. Cloned his mannerisms. Drew strong from his sacrifice. Quoted his quotes. Knocked off his name brand. Claimed I was a child of God. Would he be pissed off?   Or would he say, "Come follow me, and I will make you fishers of men and women." Aren't we all just trying to find our way, friends?

Maybe imitation is the best form of flattery, forcing us to discover innovative ways to draw love from one another.

IV.

...feelings were meant to kneel to thought as we were meant to kneel to men. But women have survived. As poets. And there are no new pains. We have felt them all already. We have hidden that fact in the same place where we have hidden our power. They lie in our dreams, and it is our dreams that point the way to freedom. They are made realizable through our poems that give us the strength and courage to see, to feel, to speak, and to dare.

~Audre Lorde, "Poetry is Not a Luxury"

AN AFFIRMATION

An affirmation is a strong, positive statement that
something is already so.
~Pamela Vaull Starr

I am a poet.

This is what I do
I affirm this to be true
I admit it to you
I confess it
I profess it
In this moment I accept it. I own it.
That I am a certified, bona fide, prophesied,
prolific Poet with a capital P
Yeah, that's me!

Get ready   Stand back
Brace yourself
as I slowly and dramatically unfasten
each silver button of my overcoat
Cover your eyes so as not to be blinded
as I tear open my super metaphorical skin
to reveal my Potent, Powerful, Primordial,
Passionate, Playful, Peaceful, Productive,
Plentiful, Positive, Palpable, Possible,
Probable, Primo, Perfecto Capital .... F???

You've got to be kidding me!
You mean to tell me that when I finally affirm,

admit, confess, profess, accept, own, that I am
indeed a certified, bona fide, prophesied Poet
with a capital P,
in turn I am burned with a Fickle, Fragile, Fake,
Fallible, Funky-Feeling, Facade of a Flippin'
Failure of a capital F frozen to my chest with
Fear?

What the F?

Breath
Breath

My inner P pacifies
and peacefully passionately ponders the
precarious position of a Powerful Potent P being
cursed with a Fallible, Finicky, Fickle,
Flippin' F stands for Fail frozen to her chest.
Why me?
Am I no more than a pathetic perpetual pretender
to poetic perfection?
I profoundly and poignantly plea with my big P:
What would a certified, bona fide
prophesied Poet do in a predicament like this one
be?

What do real capital Ps do when they are F***ed?

And then it came to me
like flame through me
like flash going off in me
I could now see clearly
that she, a real capital P

would take that F and say—
F it!
I'm gonna have fun with it
get freaky deaky with it
make others fiend for it
finesse it
funkadelic it
flavor it up a bit
fill in the folds of it
find a friend in it
feed a friend with it
feel full with it
fast forward it
flow with it
find the diamonds in it
the forever in it
fear no more of it
fly high above it
expose the world to it
frame it
and then rename it
for all the world to see
that F no longer represents the worth
others place on me
F on me stands for Free

Now I can breathe.
F for Free is so much lighter than P for Perfect.

With the lightening of my load
I lift up into the sky
spread my wings
and open my heart wide for everyone to see

that all it takes to turn an F into a P
is the fearless pen of a poet
to join the outstretched arms of an F
turning it into a P!
Ooowee…I see
and shout out
"Yeah, that's me, the one with the capital FP
plastered on her chest!
F for Free and P for Poet, spells
Freedom from Perfection
perfectly.

DANCES ANYWAY

(Inspired by Kwame Alexander's poem "Dancing Naked on the Floor," the students at Clark Academy high school, and Kate)

Write a poem that doesn't follow any rules
a poem that cheats on algebra exams
hates math and loves art
Write a poem that has an affair
with itself
a poem that dares to share a dirty secret
Write a poem where black means clean and pure
Write a poem that wears white after Labor Day
mini skirts and go-go boots any day
and purple everyday
a poem that never says,
"I'm too old to wear that."
Write a poem that sings opera in the shower,
laughs out loud in church and
cries in front of high school classmates.
Write a full-body hug poem
a poem that loves all her curves.
Write a poem that explores everything
and is ashamed of nothing
a poem that comes out of the closet
and sunbathes in the nude
Write a scared poem that writes anyway
a big bold Afro-proud poem
Write a poem that says, daaaayumn!
or at least makes me want to say damn!
an awesome, dope, crazy stupid

funky, fresh, funny, flyyyy poem.
Write a poem that soars
Write a poem that marches
for peace
not a passive poem.
Write a poem I can kiss,
console, cheer for, laugh at,
make love to, swim with.
Write a smooth poem I can rollerblade on.
Write a poem that has a beat,
a poem I can breakdance to,
dirty dance with, salsa and meringue to
a poem with rhythm.
Or write a poem that has no rhythm
like my dad—but dances anyway.
Write a poem that smells like chitlins,
collard greens, and fried chicken
a poem with soul.
Write a poem that doesn't think too much
a poem that loves to write so much
it burns dinner.
Write a poem that takes long baths
Write a lonely poem,
a poem that bleeds
Write a poem that breathes,
a poem that believes
in   something
Write a simple poem
or write a complicated double Dutch poem
a poem willing to risk getting hit by the ropes.
Write a poem that jumps in!
Write a poem that makes me want to jump in
and write my own poem.

A.R.T.

snap shot/mug shot
left profile/right profile
face showing traces of tears
frozen midstream
still cold frame
busted!
smile, you're on candid camera
exposed picking your nose
x-rays on display for everyone
to pick apart
my parts are out in the open
like a big ugly cold sore on my mouth
or in between thighs
where shame and lies reside
fester, contaminate fertility
the potential for pollination
union
I sleep topless
because it's more comfortable that way
but when I get down on my knees to pray
I put my shirt back on
can't let God see my nakedness
or have breasts hanging out
among pleads for forgiveness
so what allows me to stand in front of strangers,
friends, or you
and in the name of art
shed all of my threads?
top name brand threads
sexy, classy, trendy threads

that hug the cutting edges of my curves
and peek-a-boo only the skin
I choose to let you see
but on this platform I play
strip poker with a losing hand
every weakness I reveal about me
is a royal flush for you
I fold
and take my shirt back off
and my breasts aren't as perky
as they are in my victoria secret bra
I want to cover up my secrets
with fig leaves
hide my face like Eve
and retrieve my guise
but something keeps luring
me back to this lie detector stage
you my audience
are needles scribbling lines
like crazy on scrolling pages
when I even think I want
to lie about my frailties
with my palm   I cover lenses
that try to snap pot-shots of me
can't risk anyone seeing in color
or black and white
my bad side
my baggy eyes
my big nose
my empty bank account
or my twelve steps
towards   per   fect   ness
but in the spotlight of my fear

here I stand for A.R.T.'s sake
Art Reveals Truth.
For the sake of my truths
I stand on this stage and say
okay, go ahead
take my picture
develop my beauty
and my ugly
in a dark room
because a deep cut
must first be stitched up
and concealed
in order for it to heal
from the inside out
but eventually
you must remove the bandages
and allow the wound to be
exposed to light and air
in time,
when I tell my truths
good and bad
my scabs
fall
away
like
shame
my
    scabs
fall
    away
like

shame

MY LOVE IS

sweet
as in
a fig
not straight
forward sweet
but
complex
with its unquieted
seeds
and its
female
flesh–like
open
mouth

MY POEMS

He asks,
"What do you do with your poems?"

I reply:

I play with them. I fight with them. I flirt with
them. I avert from them. I dress up for them. I am
stripped down by them. I skinny dip into them. I
dance naked on them. Yeah, I even get jiggy wit'
em! I sing the blues out of them. I pour the joy
back into them. I open my French doors for them.
I abstain from them. I get wet waiting for them.
I am a drunken fool for them. I take twelve steps
toward them. I am sobered by them.

I carve them. I chip away at them. I get into the
grooves of them. I smooth my surfaces with them.
I accept my flaws because of them. I am flattered
by them. I am humbled in them. I am beautiful.
To them.

I stop to smell the roses with them. I notice every
detail in them. I pick them. I am pricked by them.
I bleed with them. I die in them. I ascend to
them. I am reborn through them. I birth them.

I hold hands with them. I face my fears with
them. I tremble in them. I share my secrets with
them. I share my secrets with the world through

them. I cry for the world on them. My tears are caught by them. I am baptized by them. I drown in them. I float above them. I am consoled by them. I find my soul in them. I am emboldened by them. I am subtle in them. I cuddle with them. I like to spoon with them. I become consumed by them. I taste every vowel of them. I swallow the sum of them. I drink every consonant of them. I am quenched by them.

I breathe them. I live them.

I am them.

And then

    I give them away.

JOHNS ISLAND, S.C.

If you come to my island
in the winter, in the morning
before I have opened my eyes,
before sun has risen
from inside me

If you come bearing coffee
in a reusable ceramic cup
having received
a ten percent discount
because you care
about the earth,
and our landfills,
and your footprint

And if the coffee is hot
organic, fair trade
sweet
the right color:
me with a tan

And if you place the
steamy cup on a coaster
beside my bed,
never asking me
to open my eyes

And if I smell the fingers
of the planter, and the picker

and the roaster, and the barista

And if you follow
my no-clothes-allowed rule,
shed even your socks

And if you climb in
to the other side of my bed   cold and waiting
without exposing me   to the wind

And if you look
at my pallid   naked   face
as though it were a treasure chest
my scarf-wrapped head,
a crown
And if your hand remains silent,
warmed by the holding
of a clay mug
filled with coffee
for me
And if you reach for
my palm
instead of my breast

And if you plant your stake
in this fertile ground
with intention. Claim
your home.

Consider
your   self   ship   wrecked.
You will never be free.

ABOUT THE AUTHOR

Joanna Crowell is the founder of *Ascension Theatre* and the *Women Writing from Experience* workshop series in Charleston S.C., where she facilitates creative writing workshops for women and teens and creates a platform for them to perform/share their stories. She has been a professional actress for over 20 years, having been the member of numerous theatre companies, including *Living the Dream Theatre* in Columbus, Ohio, *The African American Performance Troupe, The New American Stage Company,* and *The Actors' Theatre of South Carolina.* She has performed her own poetry across Canada and the US. At age 34, with a 9-month old baby at home, she returned to university and to her native country, Canada, in quest of incorporating more effectively women's issues and social justice and peace issues into her performance art. She now holds a BA in Women's Studies and Feminist Research and Social Justice and Peace Studies from the University of Western Ontario. She is the author of the choreopoem *Double Dutch: What are you so afraid of?* Jump in! and the play *AWOL: A Soldier's Journey* produced by *PURE Theatre* in the fall of 2011. She is a *Book-in-a-Day* and *Lowcountry Initiative for the Literary Arts* poetry coach, and currently resides in Johns Island, S.C. This is her first book.

Contact Joanna at ascendinlove@gmail.com or visit her online at www.joannacrowell.com, and "like" her at Facebook.com/JoannaCrowellArtist.

Made in the USA
San Bernardino, CA
14 February 2013